NATURE'S MYSTERIES

EARTHQUAKES

PAULA JOHANSON

Britannica Educational Publishing
IN ASSOCIATION WITH
ROSEN
EDUCATIONAL SERVICES

For Morgan, who is a mover and a shaker

Published in 2019 by Britannica Educational Publishing (a trademark of Encyclopædia Britannica, Inc.) in association with
The Rosen Publishing Group, Inc.
29 East 21st Street, New York, NY 10010

Distributed exclusively by Rosen Publishing.
To see additional Britannica Educational Publishing titles, go to rosenpublishing.com.

First Edition

Britannica Educational Publishing
J.E. Luebering: Executive Director, Core Editorial
Mary Rose McCudden: Editor, Britannica Student Encyclopedia

Rosen Publishing
Kathy Kuhtz Campbell: Senior Editor
Michael Moy: Series Designer
Tahara Anderson: Book Layout
Cindy Reiman: Photography Manager
Nicole DiMella: Photo Researcher

Library of Congress Cataloging-in-Publication Data

Names: Johanson, Paula, author.
Title: Earthquakes / Paula Johanson.
Description: New York: Britannica Educational Publishing, in Association with Rosen Educational Publishing, 2019. | Series: Nature's mysteries | Includes bibliographical references and index. | Audience: Grades 1–5.
Identifiers: LCCN 2018010039| ISBN 9781508106609 (library bound) | ISBN 9781508106487 (pbk.) | ISBN 9781508106548 (6 pack)
Subjects: LCSH: Earthquakes—Juvenile literature. | Tsunamis—Juvenile literature. | Earthquake prediction—Juvenile literature.
Classification: LCC QE521.3 .J6385 2019 | DDC 551.22—dc23
LC record available at https://lccn.loc.gov/2018010039

Manufactured in the United States of America

Photo credits: Cover, p. 1 Anadolu Agency/Getty Images; p. 4 Getty Images; pp. 5, 6, 8, 12, 15, 28 © Encyclopædia Britannica, Inc.; pp. 7, 14 Designua/Shutterstock.com; pp. 9, 10 USGS; p. 11 Gary Hincks/Science Source; p. 13 Jesse Kunerth/Shutterstock.com; p. 16 © Andrea Danti /Fotolia; p. 17 Sam Yeh/AFP/Getty Images; p. 18 Daniel Conejo/AFP/Getty Images; p. 19 Matias Delacroix/AFP/Getty Images; p. 20 NASA; p. 21 Barcroft Media/Getty Images; p. 22 Incorporated Research Institutions for Seismology; p. 23 USGS image created by Erin Burkett (USGS) and Jeff Goertzen (Orange County Register); p. 24 Pierre St. Amand/National Geophysical Data Center/NOAA; p. 25 The Asahi Shimbun /Getty Images; p. 26 Dewi Putra//Shutterstock.com; p. 27 David McNew/Getty Images; p. 29 © AP Images.; interior pages background SDubi/Shutterstock.com.

CONTENTS

WHAT ARE EARTHQUAKES?

A powerful earthquake hit eastern Alaska in 2002. When the ground shakes, roads and buildings can be damaged.

In an earthquake, huge masses of rock move beneath Earth's surface and cause the ground to shake. Earthquakes, also called temblors, are happening all the time around the world. Often, they are too small for people to feel.

Most earthquakes are caused by changes in Earth's outermost shell, or crust. The crust is made up of about a dozen masses of rock called plates. In different places, plates move

THINK ABOUT IT

Earthquakes can be frightening. Why do you think people used to wonder if the earth shaking was caused by gods or monsters?

apart, collide, or slide past each other. Over time, movement causes pressure to increase. When pressure becomes too great, the rock masses suddenly shift along a crack in the crust called a fault.

The shifting rocks release energy in the form of shock waves. These waves spread through the rock in all directions, causing an earthquake. In the most powerful quakes, people thousands of miles away can feel the ground shake.

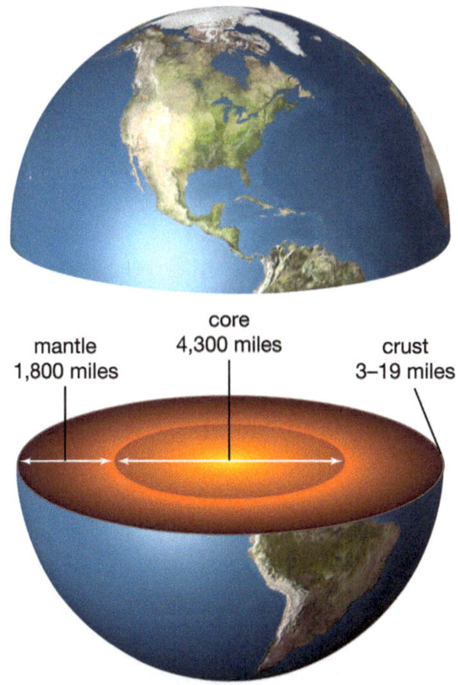

Earth has three main layers: a thin, rocky crust; a thick, rocky mantle; and a metallic core.

PLATE TECTONICS

The theory, or idea, of plate tectonics says that Earth's outer layer is made up of large, moving pieces called plates. All of Earth's land and water sit on these plates. The plates are made of solid rock. Under the plates is a weaker layer of partially melted rock. The plates are constantly moving over this weaker layer. Most plates move about 2 to 4 inches (5 to 10 centimeters) per year.

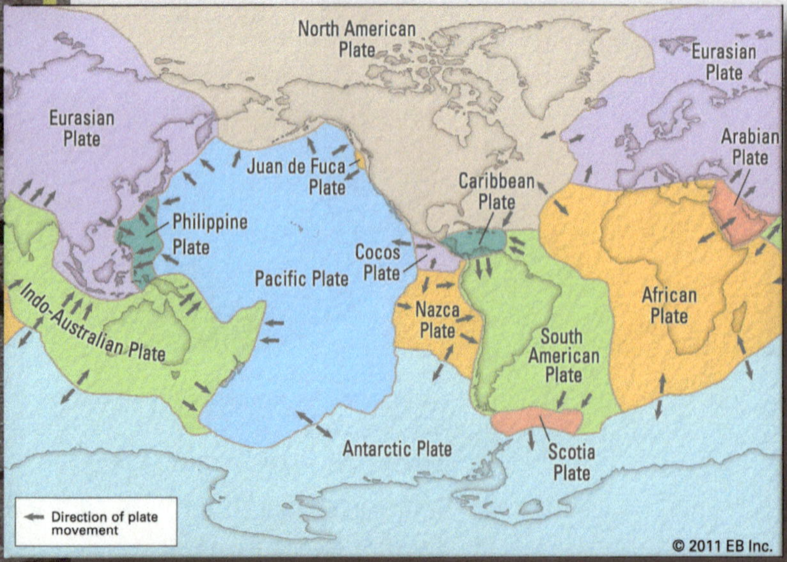

The plates that make up Earth's crust are different shapes and sizes. The map shows the direction of their movement.

COMPARE AND CONTRAST

In a pot of boiling vegetable soup, the individual vegetables move around. They rise and sink and break apart. How is a pot of soup similar to and different from Earth's crust?

As the plates move they interact at their boundaries in different ways. At one type of boundary the plates slide alongside each other. At another type the plates crash into each other. In this case, the edge of one plate may slide under another and be destroyed. Or the two edges of the plates may rise up and form mountains. At the third type of boundary the plates move apart from each other. When they do, the melted rock beneath the plates begins to rise up. This melted rock cools as it rises and forms new crust.

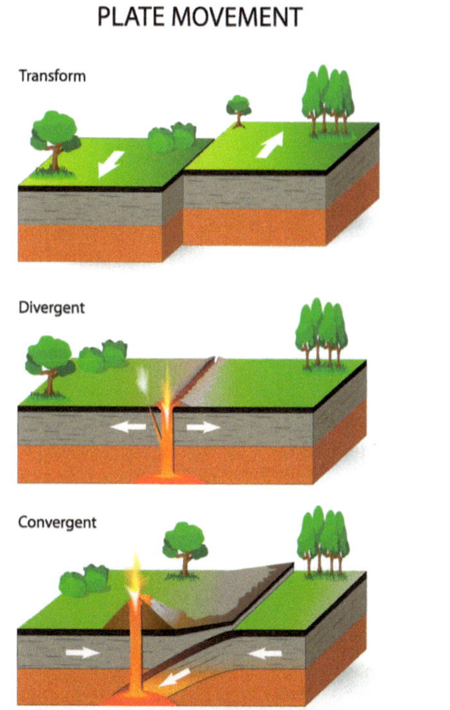

In plate movement, plates can slide past each other, move away from each other, or move toward each other.

WHERE DO EARTHQUAKES HAPPEN?

Most earthquakes take place along the boundaries of Earth's plates. One great earthquake belt circles the Pacific Ocean along the mountainous west coasts of North and South America and the island areas of Asia. It is known as the Ring of Fire. The San Andreas Fault of California is part

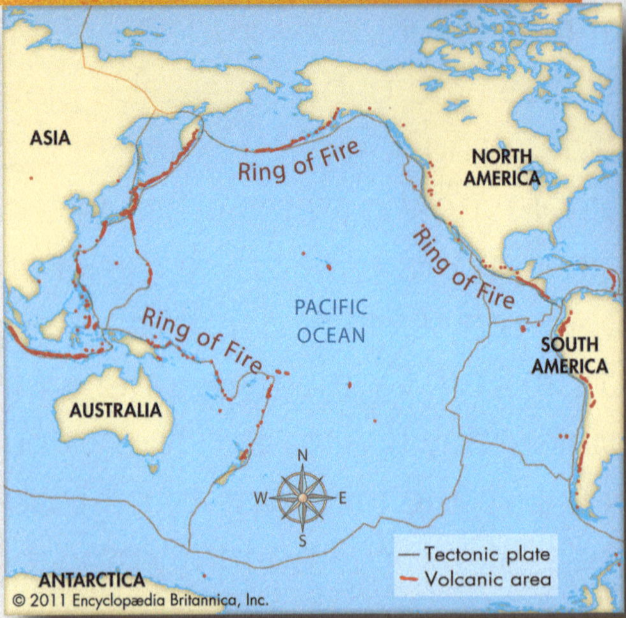

A map shows the Ring of Fire in the Pacific Ocean. It also shows the boundaries of the area's tectonic plates.

THINK ABOUT IT

The Ring of Fire is named for the chain of volcanoes that erupt in fiery explosions in a ring around the Pacific Ocean.

of this belt. A second, less-active belt is between Europe and North Africa in the Mediterranean region. It also includes parts of Asia. A small number of quakes occur in the interior of plates rather than along the edges.

Some earthquakes have other natural or human causes. Movement of melted rock in fissures beneath a volcano can trigger an earthquake. Pressure resulting from holding vast amounts of water behind large dams can cause tremors. Some quakes are caused by underground nuclear explosions and drilling for oil or gas.

The San Andreas Fault is the boundary between two major plates of Earth's crust. The plates' movements sometimes cause earthquakes.

EARTHQUAKES AND VOLCANOES

Earthquakes often occur in areas where volcanoes are found. Like earthquakes, volcanoes result from the movement of Earth's plates. Hot gases and melted rock, or magma, from deep within Earth move through cracks and faults, causing volcanic eruptions. Some violent volcanic eruptions take place where the edge of one plate is forced beneath the edge of another. Most volcanoes of this type are found around the edges of the plates under the Pacific Ocean. Fiery eruptions and earthquakes happen as the Pacific plate and the plates surrounding it grind against one another.

A severe earthquake during the eruption of Mount Saint Helens in 1980 opened a crack along the north side of the volcano.

COMPARE AND CONTRAST

Explain how earthquakes and volcanoes are similar and how they are different.

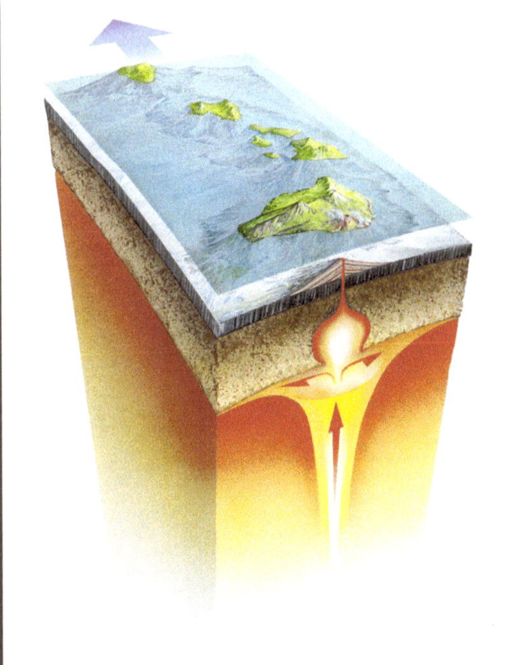

A cutaway picture shows how hot-spot volcanoes formed the islands of Hawaii.

Volcanoes also form in places where two plates slowly pull apart. This type of volcano is common along the Mid-Atlantic Ridge, a mountain chain under the Atlantic Ocean.

A small number of volcanoes are not located along the edges of plates. They form at "hot spots" in Earth's crust where melted rock rises from deep below the crust. The volcanoes of Hawaii are the best examples of hot-spot volcanoes.

EARTHQUAKES AND TSUNAMIS

Earthquakes that happen in or near oceans can cause huge, destructive waves called tsunamis to sweep ashore. A tsunami is also called a seismic sea wave. These waves travel at up to 500 miles (800 kilometers) per hour, and they can cross oceans. When a tsunami reaches a shore, it can rise as high as 100 feet (30 meters).

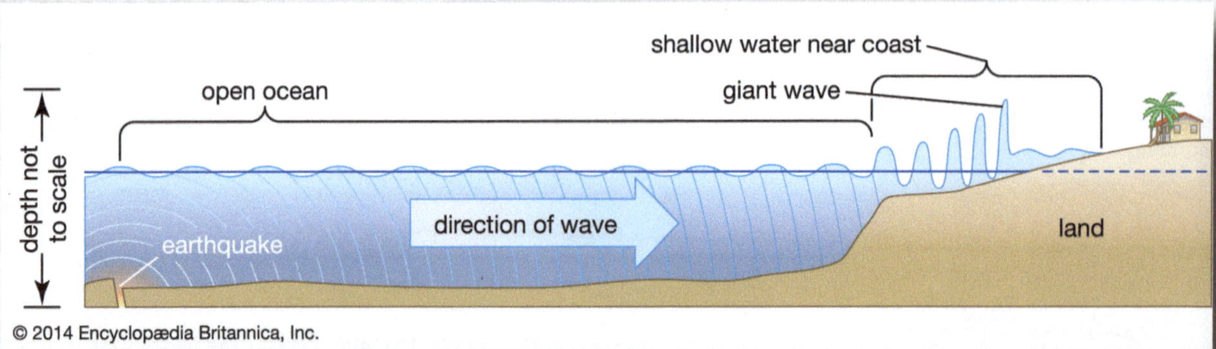

An undersea earthquake causes waves to spread out. As the waves approach a coast, they hit land under the water. This makes the waves much larger.

COMPARE AND CONTRAST

A small version of a seiche can be seen by moving a pan of water or by splashing in a bathtub of water. How do you think a seiche is similar to a tsunami? How is it different?

Sometimes an earthquake or a tsunami can cause a seiche. A seiche is a standing wave that oscillates (moves back and forth between two points) on an enclosed body of water such as a lake or bay. The waves slosh back and forth in a rhythm that can last hours or a day or two.

Seiches can be dangerous to people near the shore of a lake, such as Lake Michigan.

SHOCK WAVES

Shifting rock in an earthquake causes shock waves, called seismic waves, to spread through the rock in all directions. Seismic waves spread through Earth from the starting point of an earthquake, called the focus. The point on Earth's surface immediately above the focus is called the epicenter.

There are two types of seismic waves. Body waves

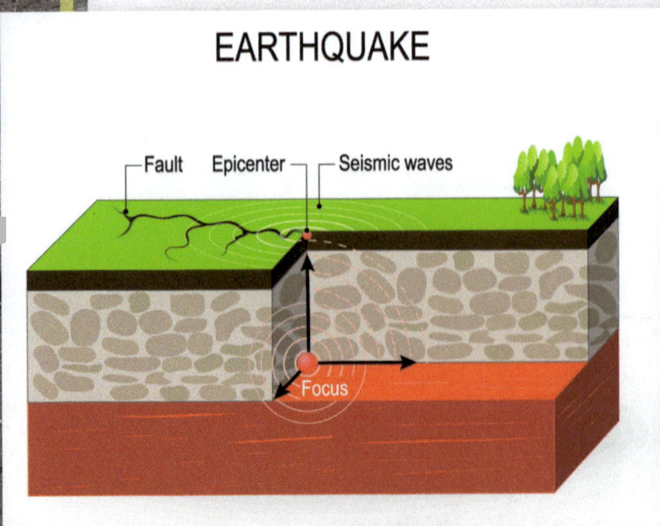

This diagram shows how an earthquake's shock waves (also called seismic waves) spread from the focus to the epicenter and beyond.

THINK ABOUT IT

Sometimes animals can feel the body waves of an earthquake before humans do. Why do you think that happens?

travel deep within the body of Earth. They are followed by surface waves, which travel along Earth's surface. Surface waves cause most of the damage during earthquakes. They travel more slowly than body waves. Some of them move the ground from side to side. Others move the ground up and down, similar to rolling waves on an ocean.

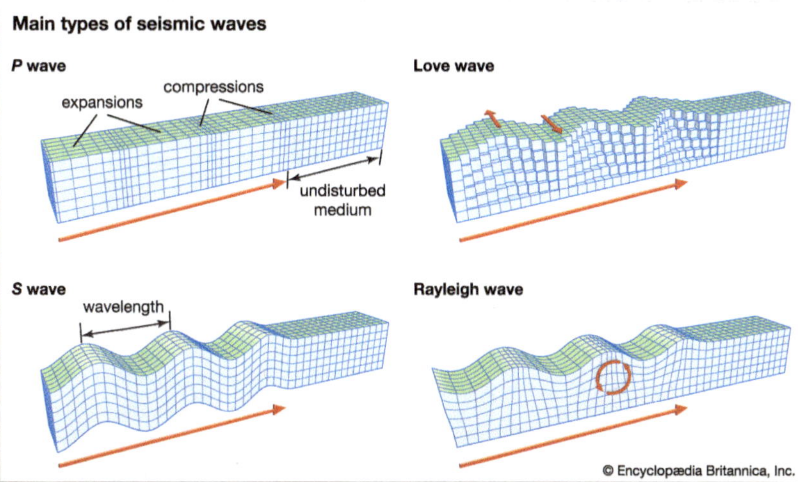

Seismic waves are body waves (labeled *P* and *S* waves in this diagram) or surface waves (labeled Love and Rayleigh waves).

MEASURING EARTHQUAKES

Seismology is the study of earthquakes and the spreading of seismic waves within Earth. Scientists called seismologists record the shock waves produced in an earthquake using an instrument called a seismograph. These records have allowed seismologists to discover a lot of information about the interior of the planet.

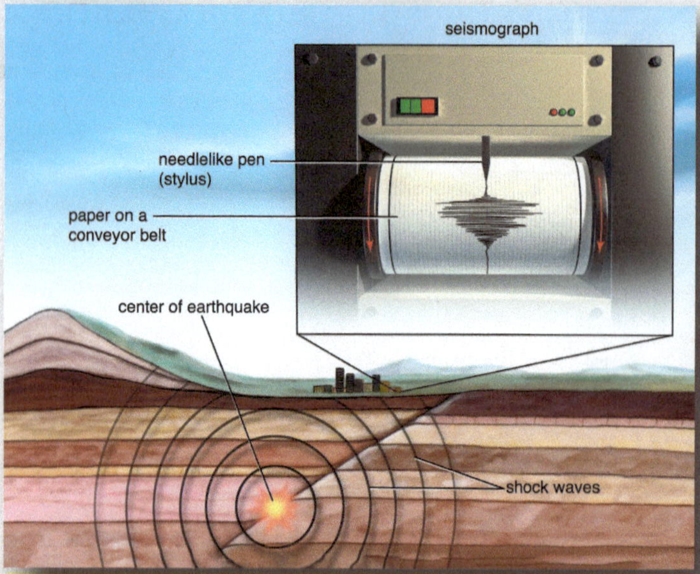

As a seismograph moves back and forth with the ground during an earthquake, a pen records the movement on a roll of paper.

The strength of a quake is measured in dif-

THINK ABOUT IT

Why would it be helpful to know when an earthquake might take place?

ferent ways. The Richter scale measures earthquakes based on the amount of energy released by rock movements. Weak earthquakes are close to zero on this scale. The strongest earthquakes measure about 9. The strongest earthquake ever measured was a 9.5. The Mercalli scale measures the amount of destruction caused by an earthquake on a scale of 1 to 12.

Seismologists keep track of earthquakes, tremors, and signs of volcanic activity. They try to predict when an earthquake or eruption might take place and how severe it will be.

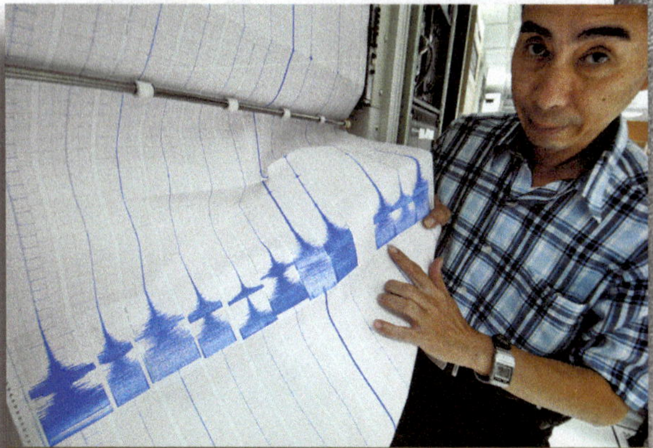

A seismologist in Taiwan measured a 2007 earthquake as being 6.6 on the Richter scale.

FORESHOCKS, AFTERSHOCKS, AND SWARMS

Most earthquakes occur without warning. Some major earthquakes are preceded by minor tremors called foreshocks. Foreshocks can come a few hours or days before the big one.

Sometimes a large earthquake is followed by a similar one along the same fault source within an hour or perhaps a day.

On April 1, 2010, areas in Mexico's state of Baja California experienced foreshocks. Three days later a powerful earthquake hit the region.

COMPARE AND CONTRAST

How might a person's reaction to an aftershock be the same as their reaction to a foreshock? How might it be different?

Usually a major earthquake is followed by one or more smaller earthquakes. These weaker earthquakes are called aftershocks. They strike along the same fault within an hour or a day. The first earthquake of a series is usually much more severe than the aftershocks. A thousand or more aftershocks might come during the first days after a big quake.

Aftershocks occurred in Culverden, New Zealand, after an earthquake damaged the town in 2016.

Large numbers of small earthquakes may occur in a region for months without a major earthquake. Such series of earthquakes are called earthquake swarms. They are often too small to feel. A few

VOCABULARY

Casualties are people who are injured or killed during an accident or disaster.

A swarm of tremors was measured in Yellowstone National Park around the first week of January in 2009.

temblors may be as strong as a 5 on the Richter scale. These might be big enough to cause property damage, but there are usually few human **casualties**.

An almost continuous tremor usually accompanies a volcano erupting with lava and hot gases. Earthquakes associated with volcanic activity often occur in swarms. Earthquake swarms are very common in Yellowstone

Sapphire Pond in Yellowstone National Park is heated by an underground volcano and shaken by tremors.

National Park, an area of high volcanic activity. It is common for the park to experience hundreds of earthquakes a month. However, swarms have also occurred in many areas with no volcanoes. Seismologists keep careful records to learn what they can about why seismic events are happening.

EARTHQUAKE PREDICTION AND WARNING SYSTEMS

Seismologists try to predict earthquakes. They share information collected by networks of seismographs. Seismologists study changes in the earth around earthquake-prone areas. These changes include crustal changes in fault zones and in rocks. Location, time, and strength of earthquakes give important clues to both tectonic and volcanic activity, particularly volcanic eruptions that are about to happen.

Seismic stations located around the world measure seismic waves and share information.

Many countries and regions have earthquake warning systems. ShakeAlert Earthquake Early Warning System is the one used for the West Coast of the United States. The United States Geological Survey (USGS)

THINK ABOUT IT

By comparing arrival times of different waves, seismologists learn the location of an earthquake many thousands of miles away. Why do they care what happens far away?

has an Earthquake Hazards Program. It monitors and reports earthquakes, examines impacts and hazards, and performs research. In 2016, the USGS issued its first one-year forecast of damaging quakes in the continental United States.

There are now international tsunami warning systems, too. When seismologists detect earthquakes on the ocean floor or the ocean coast, they share the news with places that will be in danger of tsunamis.

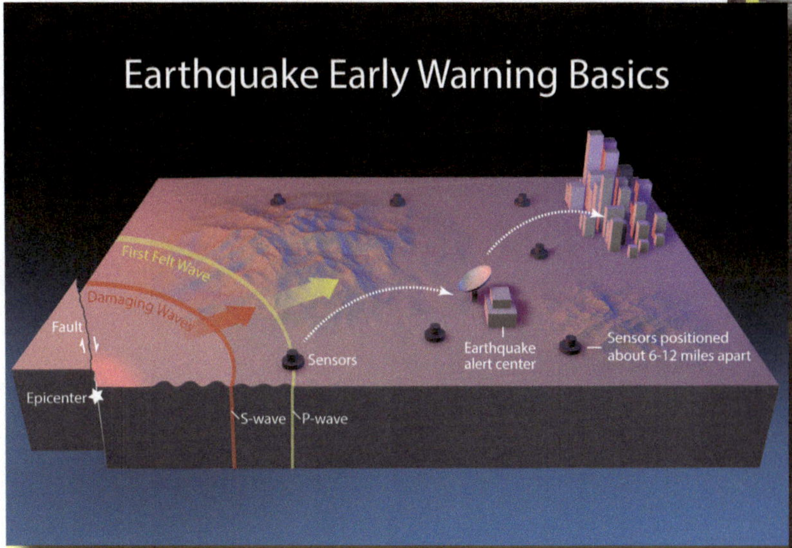

A diagram shows how a warning system such as ShakeAlert Earthquake Early Warning System can operate. Warnings can be sent quickly to a computer or phone.

DAMAGE FROM EARTHQUAKES

An earthquake may be powerful enough to change the surface of Earth, thrusting up cliffs and opening huge cracks in the ground. Amazing amounts of energy are suddenly released. The Chile earthquake of 1960 was the largest earthquake recorded in the twentieth century. It was so huge that it vibrated Earth like a guitar string! It measured 9.5 on the Richter scale and caused great damage.

The Chile earthquake of 1960 destroyed these homes. It also caused tsunamis that damaged distant Pacific coastal areas.

VOCABULARY

Avalanches are large masses of snow that quickly slide down mountainsides or over cliffs.

Earthquakes can destroy buildings, bridges, railways, and roads. They can also lead to terrible fires. Earthquakes can ruin power plants, water pipes, and dams. Tsunamis can destroy harbor docks and boats and cause floods. It can take years for a city to rebuild from earthquake damage.

An earthquake caused a landslide to destroy a bridge and roads in Kumamoto, Japan, in 2016.

Violent shaking during earthquakes often causes other Earth movements, such as tilting, landslides, and **avalanches**. Shaking can also affect wet or sandy ground, making soft mud where buildings and trees can sink or fall.

EARTHQUAKE SAFETY

After a 2006 earthquake in Java, these dome-shaped homes were built to resist damage from tremors.

There is no way to prevent an earthquake from happening. There are ways, however, to avoid some of the damage that earthquakes can cause. Many cities in earthquake zones have rules for building houses and other structures. The buildings have to be made strong enough to survive powerful shaking. People in such areas also prepare for earthquakes in other ways. They may keep supplies of food and water nearby. They also practice what to do if there is an earthquake.

THINK ABOUT IT

If you are outdoors when you feel the shaking of an earthquake, where do you think you should go to be safe until the shaking stops?

The United States Department of Homeland Security recommends that people know the safety exercise Drop, Cover, and Hold On! The exercise instructs people to drop to the ground; cover their heads and necks with their arms to protect themselves from falling objects indoors; and to hold on to any sturdy covering until the shaking stops. Other instructions include staying away from windows or anything that could fall and remaining indoors until the shaking stops.

These students are learning to protect themselves during an earthquake drill at their school.

EARTHQUAKES MAKE HISTORY

There have been many big earthquakes that damaged cities and killed thousands of people. Most of those were in areas that are near the edges of tectonic plates. Others have been in unexpected areas. In 1811 and 1812, there were three powerful earthquakes in Missouri. Their **magnitude** was at least 7.5 on the Richter scale.

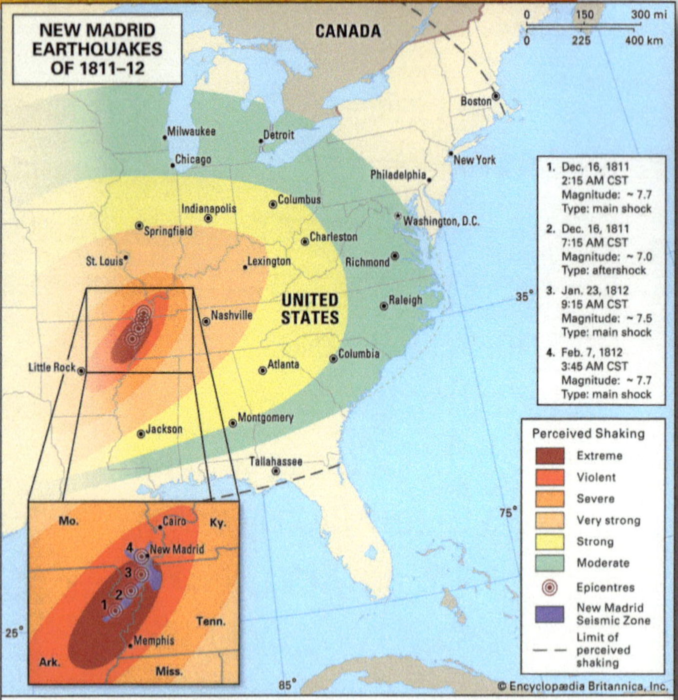

Note: Modern city locations and state boundaries shown.
Sources: Magnitude and time of earthquakes from U.S. Geological Survey, Earthquake Hazards Program, "New Madrid 1811–1812 Earthquakes." Perceived shaking information from Otto W. Nuttli, "The Mississippi Valley Earthquakes of 1811 and 1812" (1973); and U.S. Geological Survey.

A map shows the location and strength of the earthquakes in New Madrid, Missouri, in 1811–12.

VOCABULARY

The magnitude of an earthquake is a measurement on the Richter scale of how much energy was released.

A massive earthquake off the coast of Japan in March 2011 caused a series of huge tsunami waves. At least twenty thousand people were killed. Places all around the world, from Pakistan to New Zealand to Mexico, have suffered major earthquakes as well.

Earthquakes are becoming more frequent in many areas. Humans are now causing some earthquakes by drilling for oil and gas. Since the early 2000s the state of Oklahoma and the province of Alberta in Canada have experienced an increase in the number and strength of earthquakes because of drilling.

Drilling for oil and gas in Sparks, Oklahoma, is believed to have triggered an earthquake that ruined homes.

GLOSSARY

BODY WAVES Seismic waves that travel through Earth's interior.

EARTHQUAKE ZONE An area where earthquakes are common and expected.

FAULT A break in Earth's crust where masses of rock move parallel to the break.

FISSURE A narrow opening or crack.

LANDSLIDE The slipping down of a mass of rocks or earth on a steep slope.

LAVA Melted rock that flows out of volcanoes or other openings in the surface of Earth.

MAGMA Rock melted inside Earth.

METALLIC Made of metal or containing metal.

PLATE A part of Earth's surface; a piece of the rocky outer crust.

TREMOR A slight shaking movement of the ground before or after an earthquake.

VIBRATE To move back and forth or from side to side rapidly so as to produce a quivering effect or sound.

VOLCANO An opening in Earth's crust where hot gases and melted rock from deep within Earth find their way up to the surface. A sudden explosion of a volcano is called an eruption.

FOR MORE INFORMATION

Books

Brooks, Susie. *Earthquakes and Volcanoes* (Where on Earth?). New York, NY: PowerKids Press, 2017.

Prager, Ellen J., and Susan Greenstein. *Earthquakes* (Jump into Science). Washington, DC: National Geographic Society, 2017.

Wagstaffe, Johanna. *Fault Lines: Understanding the Power of Earthquakes.* Victoria, BC: Orca Book Publishers, 2017.

Winchester, Simon. *When the Earth Shakes: Earthquakes, Volcanoes, and Tsunamis*. New York, NY: Viking, 2015.

Websites

National Geographic Kids

Earthquake

https://kids.nationalgeographic.com/explore/science/earthquake

Ready: Earthquakes

https://www.ready.gov/earthquakes

UPSeis Michigan Tech Geological Education Site

http://www.geo.mtu.edu/UPSeis/index.html

US Geological Survey's Earthquake Hazards Program

Earthquakes for Kids

https://earthquake.usgs.gov/learn/kids/

Facebook: @USGeologicalSurvey

Twitter: @USGSEarthquakes

INDEX